new sushi

Emi Kazuko

new sushi

PHOTOGRAPHY BY Gus Filgate

jacqui
small

dedication

To my late parents who provided me with a good foundation in life and food

acknowledgements

I would like to thank the late Kenneth Lo and my long time friend Dehta Hsiung, who introduced me, at different stages of my writing career, to the joy of writing cookery books in English. My heartfelt thanks also go to all my dear friends in Japan as well as abroad who keep me informed of any new development in Japanese food, especially to Katsuko Hirose for her unceasing willingness to assist in research from Japan, Katsu Yoshino for his incomparable knowledge of the world food scene and Atsuko Console who also very efficiently assisted me with the cooking for the photography for this book. I would like to thank my editor, Madeline Weston, for her painstaking editing, Gus Filgate for his magnificent photography, Valerie Fong, for her beautiful design and, above all, the publisher Jacqui Small for giving me the opportunity to write this book.

First published in 2005 by Jacqui Small, an imprint of Aurum Press Ltd, 25 Bedford Avenue, London WC1B 3AT

Text copyright © Emi Kazuko 2006
Photography, design and layout copyright © Jacqui Small 2006

PUBLISHER Jacqui Small
EDITORIAL MANAGER Kate John
ART DIRECTOR Valerie Fong
PHOTOGRAPER Gus Filgate
PROPS STYLIST Penny Markham
EDITOR Madeline Weston
PRODUCTION Peter Colley

Knives from The Japanese Knife Company www.japaneseknifecompany.com

ISBN 1 903221 65 X

A catalogue record for this book is available from the British Library.
2008 2007 2006
10 9 8 7 6 5 4 3 2 1

PRINTED IN CHINA

contents

introduction   06

the basics   08

soups   12

maki-zushi   14

nigiri-zushi   32

oshi-zushi, chirashi
    and others   42

glossary + index   64

introduction

Sushi was Japan's answer to the sandwich, perfect mouthfuls of food that could be eaten on a range of occasions. It is now hugely popular in all countries of the world and is ideal food for parties or lunch snacks, picnics or celebrations. It is infinitely adaptable and can be both casual and stylish; the ingredients can be either the authentic Japanese choices or fusion sushi, using the ingredients of other countries and cultures.

Sushi, once regarded as the ultimate mysterious Japanese cuisine, made its sensational international debut in the late Eighties with the introduction of *kaiten-zushi* (literally, 'going-round sushi') for the first time outside Japan. Its popularity has since grown to the extent of creating a sushi phenomenon all over the world. In this millennium century its popularity has continued to grow until it has reached every corner of the world. I have witnessed, from New York to Moscow and Sydney to Stockholm, that sushi is no longer an unfamiliar food, but is adopted by people everywhere, using their local produce and creating new fusion sushi along the way. I see this happening to my favourite food wherever I go, just when I have been most active in my own personal efforts to introduce Japanese cuisine to the world: I feel very excited and privileged indeed.

Sushi has many faces: at the top, exclusive sushi restaurants, where you sit in front of the master chef and are expected to know the manners of a connoisseur, it's like a precious little art work (with a price to match); it can be a banquet food for weddings and festivals; a family meal at restaurants or at home to mark occasions such as birthdays, christenings and funerals; a picnic for outings, sports days and theatre;

a quick lunch or snack to take away, and of course it's served on a conveyer belt. Sushi is in a class of its own: it's very stylish yet quite casual at the same time, and sushi excites people – even us Japanese who have been eating it all our lives – for its shape, colour and tastes, above all for its sheer uniqueness. In short it is a diverse, friendly food, and that's what gives it its global appeal.

And sushi is a complete food: nutritionally sound and healthy, unlike most other snack foods. In a tiny bite-sized morsel, it contains all the fundamental nutrients: carbohydrate, protein and vitamins among others. It is also not only easy but fun to make at home. Sushi chefs certainly look the happiest people in the restaurant world, simply because they enjoy making sushi so much! Sushi is not only my favourite food to eat out, but also to entertain my friends, and I have very much enjoyed making such a wide range of sushi for this book.

I have tried to capture the diversity of this jewel of Japanese cuisine, bearing in mind that the ultra freshness necessary for fish to be eaten absolutely raw has to be carefully sourced outside Japan. I do hope you will join me in the fun of making sushi.

sushi utensils and ingredients

sushi utensils

1 *handai* (wooden *sumeshi* tub), **fan** (for cooling the rice), **rice paddle** 2 *oshi-zushi* **press** (for pressed sushi) 3 **knives** (vegetable, *sashimi*, general purpose) 4 *makisu* (bamboo sushi mat in full and half-roll sizes), **wooden spatula** 5 *hashi* (Japanese chopsticks) 6 *tamago-yaki* **pan** (Japanese omelette pan)

sushi ingredients

1 **shiitake mushrooms** (dried) 2 **fried tofu** (for *inari* sushi) 3 *hijiki* (dried seaweed) 4 *nori* (seeweed sheets) 5 *konbu* (dried kelp) 6 **rice** (short grain) 7 **white sesame seeds** 8 **black sesame seeds** 9 *takuan* (pickled daikon) 10 **ginger root** 11 *sake* 12 *shoyu* 13 **vinegar** 14 *mirin*

how to **cut fish**
Holding the knife at a slight angle, cut the fillet slightly diagonally in one firm action by drawing the knife towards you.

how to **skin fish**
Separate the skin and the flesh at one end of the fish, and holding the skin down on the board, insert the blade of a sharp knife at a slight angle between the skin and flesh. Draw the knife blade along the skin.

how to **peel the filament from skin**
Using your fingers, carefully separate the filament from the skin at the head end of the fish and pull back towards the tail.

how to cook **vegetables**

Dried shiitake
To cook 5 dried shiitake:
100ml shiitake soaked liquid
1 tablespoon sugar
1/4 teaspoon salt
2 tablespoons *shoyu*
1 tablespoon *mirin*
1 tablespoon *sake*

Soak the dried shiitake in water overnight or at least 1 hour. Drain, retaining the liquid, and cut the shiitake into fine strips. In a saucepan, mix the measured shiitake liquid with the other ingredients and bring to a boil over a moderate heat, stirring until the sugar has dissolved. Add the shiitake and simmer over low heat for about 10 minutes until soft. Remove from the heat and leave to cool in the liquid until ready to use.

---

how to **devein prawns** and **keep prawns straight while cooking**

1 Pull the head from a prawn with your fingers, and insert a cocktail stick through a gap in the shell from the side.

2 Pick up the vein with the cocktail stick and using your fingers very gently pull it out.

To keep the prawns straight while cooking, insert the cocktail stick through the body. They should be as cooked in their shells as briefly as possible.

Dried *hijiki* seaweed
Soak in plenty of water for 30 minutes; dried *hijiki* expands to about 5 times in volume. Drain and, and if long, cut into 1–2cm long pieces. Cook in the same liquid used for shiitake.

Carrot
Chop into fine matchsticks. Drain and cook in the same liquid as used for cooking shiitake, just to cover the carrot. Alternatively use fish or vegetable stock.

---

vinegared ginger
100g ginger
FOR THE MARINADE:
100ml rice vinegar
50ml water
2 1/2 tablespoons sugar

Using a fine mandolin or peeler, very finely slice the ginger and cook in boiling water over a medium heat for 2 minutes. Drain and pat dry with a kitchen paper. Mix the rice vinegar, water and sugar and stir until the sugar has dissolved. Marinate the ginger for 5–6 days. It will keep for months in the refrigerator.

pink radish flower

Trim a radish and place upright on a board between 2 *hashi* or pencils, and make deep cross cuts until the blade touches the *hashi*. Sprinkle with salt and leave for 20–30 minutes. Squeeze out the excess moisture. Make the vinegar marinade (see Vinegared ginger, page 9) and marinate the radish overnight. The red of the radish colours the whole flower shape pink.

1,2 cucumber 3 carrot 4 *takuan* (pickled daikon) 5 daikon 6 shiitake mushroom 7 *wasabi* powder and paste 8 ginger root and slices 9 radishes, plain and pickled

making *sumeshi* (sushi rice)

Cooking rice is not only the starting point of the sushi making but also the most important part of any Japanese cooking. Sushi chefs spend years training but with a little care the basic technique is quickly mastered.

When boiling rice in a saucepan over a direct heat you need to cook at least 1 cup (225g) of rice to get a good result for making sushi. A cup of rice will make about 450g of cooked rice, and this will make approximately 6 thin rolls (6–8 pieces per roll), enough to serve 4 persons as a starter. Most of the recipes in this book use this amount of rice.

1 cup (225g) rice
250–300ml water

FOR THE VINEGAR DRESSING:
2²⁄₃–3 tablespoons ready-made
   sushi vinegar or 2 tablespoons
   Japanese rice vinegar or white
   wine vinegar
1½ teaspoons sugar (2 teaspoons
   if using wine vinegar)
½ teaspoon salt

1 Wash the rice thoroughly, changing the water several times until it is clear, and leave to drain in a strainer for at least 30 minutes, ideally 1 hour. Absorbing water slowly makes the rice evenly milky white in colour.

2 Place the rice in a large, deep saucepan and add the water; the water should not come higher than a third of the depth. Cover and bring to the boil on a medium heat – about 5 minutes. Lower the heat to the minimum and, using a wooden spatula, quickly stir the rice from top to bottom. Cover and slowly simmer on a very low heat for 9–10 minutes until the water has been absorbed but bubbles are still forming on top of the rice. Lightly turn the rice over from bottom to top with the spatula, and continue to simmer, covered, for another 1 minute. Remove from the heat, and leave to stand, covered, for 10 minutes.

3 If not using the ready mixed sushi vinegar, mix the rice vinegar, sugar and salt for in a cup and stir until dissolved.

4 Transfer the hot rice to a *handai* (wooden *sumeshi* tub) or a non-metallic mixing bowl. Sprinkle the vinegar dressing over and, using the spatula, fold the vinegar mixture into the rice – do not stir. Quickly cool the rice using a fan while folding and when hot enough to handle, use to make sushi.

making *tamago-yaki* (thick omelette)

1 Sieve the beaten eggs to break up the whites and mix with the sugar, *shoyu* and a pinch of salt, stirring until the sugar has dissolved.

2 Heat a rectangular *tamago-yaki* pan or a small frying pan, about 14cm in diameter, over moderate heat and pour the oil evenly into the pan. (Use a non-stick pan to avoid the oiling altogether.) Using kitchen paper, wipe off excess oil. Lower the heat and pour about a quarter of the egg evenly into the pan. Prick any air bubbles with a fork.

3 When the egg is about to set, roll the egg 3–4 times from one side to the other. Oil the empty part of the pan with the oiled paper, and push the rolled egg to the other side. Oil the pan again, and pour in another quarter of the egg. Again roll the egg using the first roll as the centre. Repeat this oiling and rolling twice more.

4 Remove from the pan, and when cool cut into the required shape and size.

---

tamago-yaki (thick omelette)

Makes 1 log shaped omelette (about 14 x 5 x 5cm)

4 eggs, beaten
1 tablespoon sugar
1 teaspoon *shoyu* (soy sauce)
salt
2 tablespoons vegetable oil

tamago-usuyaki (thin egg sheet)

Makes 1 sheet (20cm diameter)

1 egg, beaten
salt
vegetable oil

Sieve the beaten egg, or break the lumpy white with a fork and add a little salt. Heat a frying pan, about 20cm diameter, and add a little vegetable oil, then spread over the pan with a kitchen paper. Lower the heat, then pour in the beaten egg and spread evenly by tilting the pan. Cook each side for 30 seconds or until just dry, and remove from the heat. When cool cut into the required shape and size. (Use a non-stick pan to avoid the oiling.)

miso soup with tofu and *nameko*

Serves 4

600ml water
1 piece (about 10 x 10cm) *konbu*
   (dried kelp)
30g *hanakatsuo/kezuribushi*
   (dried bonito flakes) or 1 sachet
   powdered *dashi* (soup stock) or
   ½ teaspoon *dashi* granules
5g dried *wakame* or 50g spinach
2 tablespoons red *miso* (soya paste)
½ cake (150g) tofu, cut into small dices
1 tin (85g) cooked *nameko* mushrooms
1 spring onion, finely shredded

1 To make an authentic *dashi* (fish stock) put the water and *konbu* in a saucepan and bring to a boil over moderate heat and just before starting bubbling remove the *konbu* and discard. Add the *hanakatsuo* and cook for 4–5 minutes on a low heat. Remove from the heat and leave until the *hanakatsuo* has settled to the bottom of the pan. Sieve the *dashi* through a cloth. Alternatively, dilute powdered or granulated *dashi* in the boiling water.

2 Soak the *wakame* in plenty of water for 10 minutes, drain and using your hands squeeze out the excess water. Chop into small pieces. If using spinach, chop into bite-size pieces.

3 Dilute the *miso* in a cup with some of the *dashi* stock from the pan and return to the pan. Add the *wakame* or spinach, tofu and *nameko* and heat over a moderate heat. Just before boiling remove from the heat and serve in individual soup bowls garnished with the spring onion on top.

---

ushio-jiru (clear soup with clams)

Serves 4

1 piece (10 x 10cm) *konbu* (dried kelp),
   cleaned
2 tablespoons *sake*
600ml water
4 large fresh clams in shells, cleaned
⅔ teaspoon salt
½ cake tofu (150g), cut into 12 cubes
4 springs *mitsuba* (Japanese parsley)
   or watercress

1 Put the *konbu*, *sake* and water in a saucepan and leave for 20 minutes.

2 Add the clams to the saucepan and bring to a boil over a high heat. Just before it reaches boiling, remove the *konbu* and discard. Lower the heat and simmer on a moderate heat, spooning off the scum that rises to the surface, until all the clams open up. Season with the salt.

3 Add the tofu and bring back to near boiling point, add the *mitsuba* or watercress and immediately remove from the heat. Arrange a clam and 3 cubes of tofu in each of 4 individual soup bowls and pour the soup over. Serve garnished with a sprig of the wilted *mitsuba* or watercress on top.

miso soup with tofu and nameko

Miso is used daily in the Japanese household, but is most commonly used for this soup. Almost anything goes in the soup, but here one of the increasingly popular and available mushrooms, nameko, is used. Cooked and tinned nameko is available at Japanese supermarkets. There are many types of miso on the market, but red, strong miso goes well with nameko and tofu.

ushio-jiru (clear soup with clams)

Nothing is more soothing than a bowl of hot soup at the end of a sushi session, and an alternative to the usual miso soup is a clear soup. Ushio, old word for sea tide, uses clams as the main ingredient as well as for the soup stock. Either steaming with sake or simmering in soup as in this recipe are the best way to appreciate the fresh clams' natural flavour and texture.

maki-zushi (rolled sushi)

Maki-zushi or *norimaki* (*nori* rolled sushi) started life as ideal for picnics, just like sandwiches in the West. It's now a synonym outside Japan for sushi itself, and many varieties have been invented all over the world, using numerous local ingredients.

traditional *hosomaki* (thin rolls) **with three colours**

Here the technique of *norimaki* is explained using three ingredients of
different colours. TRADITIONAL *HOSOMAKI* IS SHOWN ON PAGE 14 ON THE LEFT.

Makes 6 rolls
  (2 each colour, cut into 48 pieces) to
  serve 4 people as a starter

1 quantity sushi rice (see page 10)
18cm cucumber
1 small tuna or salmon fillet
  (about 200g)
18cm *takuan* (pickled daikon)
3 sheets *nori* (20 x 18cm), cut into half
  (10 x 18cm)
wasabi paste
2 tablespoons white sesame seeds,
  lightly toasted
4 *shiso* leaves, finely shredded, optional

FOR THE HAND VINEGAR:
1 cup (250ml) water
2 tablespoons rice vinegar

TO SERVE:
vinegared ginger (see page 8)
shoyu (soy sauce)

1 Make the sushi rice. Meanwhile, prepare the filling ingredients. Quarter the cucumber lengthways and cut out the seeds. Using two of the pieces, with the skin on, make 2 cucumber sticks, 1cm square; use the rest for salad. Cut the tuna (or salmon, skinned) into 1cm square pieces. You will need a total length of about 40cm. Cut the *takuan* to get 2 sticks, similar to the cucumber.

2 Place a *makisu* (bamboo sushi mat) in parallel with you, and place half a *nori* sheet sideways, as in Step 1 opposite. With hands wetted in the hand vinegar, take a sixth of the sushi rice (about 70g) in your hands, and mould as in Step 2 opposite and place on the *nori*.

3 Spread the rice and add some more rice to fill any gaps to cover the *nori* evenly, leaving about 2cm margin at the far side. (Step 2.)

4 Take a tiny amount of *wasabi* paste on the tip of your finger, and spread in a line across the centre of the rice. Place a stick of cucumber across on top of the *wasabi* and place 1 tablespoon sesame seeds alongside.

5 Roll the *makisu* as in Step 3 opposite, keeping the cucumber in the centre with your fingers. Lift the upper edge of the *makisu*, and roll the rice cylinder onto the rest of the *nori*. Cover the rolled sushi with the mat and gently press into a nice round shape. Remove from the mat, and keep in a flat container, the join side down. Cover with a dry tea towel while making the remaining rolls. Repeat this rolling using the remaining cucumber and sesame seeds.

6 Make 2 more rolls with tuna instead of cucumber, and a further 2 with *takuan* with *shiso* shreds. With the *takuan*, do not use the *wasabi* because *takuan* is already strongly flavoured. Cut each roll into 8, and arrange cut side up on a serving plate. Serve with vinegared ginger and a small dish of *shoyu*.

how to roll *maki-zushi*

1 Toast the *nori* very briefly, about 10cm above a low heat, before use particularly if the *nori* is not very crispy. This makes it crispy and also brings out the flavour. Then place a sheet of *nori*, shiny side down on the *makisu*.

2 With hands wetted in the hand vinegar, mould a portion of rice into a cylinder. Put it on the *nori* about 2cm away from the far edge. Using the tip of your fingers, spread the rice towards you. Place the fillings on the bed of rice.

3 Pick up the *makisu* from the near side, and roll over, keeping the filling in the centre with your fingers, and joining the rice together with the rice inside the *nori*. Gently press into a nice round shape. Remove from the mat.

tri-colour *maki* a l'Italia (three colour pepper roll)

Italian cooking is my favourite after Japanese, and I love all those roasted vegetables particularly peppers. This vegetarian roll is wonderful both in terms of look and taste (SHOWN ON PAGE 15 ON THE RIGHT).

Makes 6 rolls (48 pieces)

1 quantity sushi rice (see page 10)
1 green pepper
1 red pepper
1 orange/yellow pepper
1 tablespoon capers, finely chopped
salt and freshly ground black pepper
3 sheets nori (20 x 18cm), cut into half
   (10 x 18cm)

TO GARNISH:
basil and/or rocket salad
shoyu (soy sauce)

1 Make the sushi rice. While the rice is cooking prepare the peppers.

2 To peel the peppers, insert a fork through the core and grill over a flame, constantly rotating so that the skin gets lightly charred. Carefully peel the thin skin off and cut each pepper in half lengthways. Deseed and chop into approximately 5mm thick strips. Mix the pepper strips and the capers together in a bowl and season with salt and pepper.

3 Prepare a rice bed on a *nori* following the method above. Place 2 strips of each colour of peppers in a row across the centre of the rice and roll. Repeat this process to make further 5 rolls.

4 Cut each roll into 8 pieces and arrange on a serving platter garnished with some basil or rocket salad and serve the *shoyu* in individual dishes.

how to roll *uramaki-zushi* (reverse roll)

1 Cover a *makisu* with cling film. Place a sheet of *nori* crossways it, shiny side down. Wet your hands with hand vinegar (page 16) and mould a portion of rice into a cylinder, spread the rice until it covers the *nori*. Sprinkle a portion of sesame seeds over the rice.

2 Turn over the rice bed on the cling film-covered *makisu*, so the rice side is down. Put the fillings in a row across the centre of the *nori*.

3 Pick up the side of *makisu* nearest you and, keeping the filling in the centre, roll the mat over, overlapping about 1cm so that the rice sticks on to the *nori*. Roll the *norimaki* over a little inside the mat to keep the joint down. Remove the *uramaki* .

Makes 4 rolls (24 pieces)

1 quantity sushi rice (see page 10)
8 large fresh tiger prawns
plain flour
1 egg, beaten
dried breadcrumbs
vegetable oil for deep frying
2 sheets *nori* (20 x 18cm), cut into half
    (10 x 18cm)
4 tablespoons white sesame seeds,
    lightly toasted
lemon wedges
vinegared ginger (see page 8)
shoyu (soy sauce) with lemon juice

1 Make the sushi rice. Meanwhile, prepare the filling ingredients. Devein and skewer the prawns following the method on page 8, leaving the tails intact. Peel them and dust with plain flour. Dip in the egg, and roll in the dried breadcrumbs avoiding the tail. Gently press on the breadcrumbs to stick to the prawn.

2 Heat the oil to about 170°C and deep-fry the prawns for 2–3 minutes, turning once or twice until light golden, then drain on kitchen paper. When cool, remove the skewers.

3 Prepare the *uramaki-zushi* as shown above, using half a sheet of *nori*, a quarter of the sushi rice, and 1 tab lespoon of seame seeds.

4 Put 2 fried prawns in a row in the centre of the *nori*, with the tail ends to each sides, and make the *uramaki* as in Step 3 above. Repeat this process to make 3 more rolls with the remaining *nori* halves, sesame seeds and fried prawns.

5 Cut each roll into 6 pieces and arrange cut-side up on a serving plate, garnished with lemon and vinegared ginger. Serve with a little *shoyu* in individual dishes. Add lemon juice to the *shoyu* if preferred.

uramaki ebi-fry roll (reverse roll with fried prawn)

Uramaki, where the *nori* is inside and rice outside, is now a more popular form of *maki-zushi* than the traditional *nori*-outside rolls because you can use a variety of fillings without the danger of puncturing the *nori*, which makes it a lot easier to make.

california roll

This is probably the first and the most well-known 'fusion' sushi invented outside Japan, using avocado, abundant in California, and is now a fixture at most sushi shops even in Japan. Seafood sticks are usually used in this roll, but use the real thing – king crab leg meat – and taste the difference.

Makes 4 rolls (24 pieces)

1 quantity sushi rice (see page 10)
1–2 large king crab leg meat pieces, or 6 seafood sticks
1 avocado, peeled and stoned
2 *nori* sheets, halved crossways
4 tablespoons *tobiko* fish roe, or sesame seeds, lightly toasted
bunch of chives
2 tablespoons mayonnaise, optional
vinegared ginger (see page 8)
shoyu (soy sauce)
wasabi

1 Make the sushi rice. Meanwhile, prepare the filling ingredients. Cut each king crab leg meat lengthways in 2 or 4 depending on the thickness to make 4 sticks of about 'fountain pen' size. If using seafood sticks, cut in half lengthways. Cut the avocado into 8 slices lengthways.

2 Prepare a *nori* rice bed following the method for *uramaki* (page 18), and sprinkle 1 tablespoon *tobiko* (or sesame seeds) over the rice, and gently pat so that the *tobiko* sticks to the rice.

3 Turn over the whole rice bed onto the cling film-covered *makisu* in the same way as *uramaki*. Put 2 slices of avocado across in a row together with 1 piece of crab meat or 3 halves of seafood sticks. Add 6–8 sprigs of chive alongside the avocado and crab, allowing them to stick out at the ends by about 3–4cm. Spoon about ½ tablespoonful of mayonnaise, if using, on the ingredients.

4 Pick up the *makisu* from the side nearest you and roll once according to the method on page 18. Remove the California roll from the *makisu*. Repeat to make 3 more rolls with the remaining ingredients. Cut each roll into 6, and serve garnished with some vinegared ginger, *shoyu* and a little *wasabi* in a small dish.

kakiage 'spider roll' (vegetable tempura roll)

Spider roll (soft-shell crab tempura roll) is one of the more recent additions to the fusion sushi menu from abroad, and is yet to be established in Japan. Soft-shell crab tempura combined with sushi rice gives a unique appearance with crab claw meat sticking out like spider legs. As soft-shell crab is not always available, I used *kakiage* (vegetable tempura) instead and it works splendidly as shown here.

Makes 8 rolls (24 pieces)

1 quantity sushi rice (see page 10)
vegetable oil for deep-frying

FOR THE TEMPURA BATTER:
200ml ice cold water
100g plain flour
salt

1 carrot, peeled and cut into
   5–7cm x 5mm sticks
1 parsnip, peeled and cut into
   5–7cm x 5mm sticks
32 fine beans, trimmed
2 sheets *nori*, each cut into 4
8 tablespoons black sesame seeds,
   lightly toasted

TO GARNISH:
vinegared ginger (see page 8)
shoyu with lime juice

1 Make the sushi rice following the method on page 10. Meanwhile, prepare the ingredients.

2 In a deep frying pan or a wok heat the vegetable oil to about 170°C.

3 In a large bowl, mix the ice cold water (or water with some ice cubes) and the flour with a pinch of salt and using a fork, lightly stir a few times. Do not whisk; the batter should be slightly lumpy.

4 Take 2 carrot sticks, 2 parsnip sticks, and 2 fine beans and, using a slotted spoon, dip them in the batter. Then lower them into the hot oil: the batter will hold them together in a bundle. Deep-fry for 1–2 minutes, turning once or twice until soft and golden brown but still crunchy. Do not fry more than 2 bundles at one time. Drain on a wire rack or on a kitchen paper, and leave to cool.

5 Prepare a rice bed in the same way as for *uramaki* (see page 18), but use quarter of a sheet of *nori* and 1/8 of the sushi rice on each of the *nori*. Spread about a tablespoonful of the black sesame seeds all over the rice. Turn over onto the cling film-covered *makisu* vertically with the shortest sides parallel to you.

6 Put 2 pieces of the *kakiage* (vegetable tempura) crossways in a row, with 2–3 cm of the *kakiage* sticking out of the both sides, in the centre on the *nori*, and roll onto the far side. Remove from the *makisu*.

7 Repeat this process to make 7 more rolls using the remaining ingredients. Cut each roll into 3 crossways, and serve on a serving platter, garnished with vinegared ginger and *shoyu* with lime juice in individual dishes.

salmon-skin roll

Normally discarded salmon skin makes a surprisingly delicious filling. You can use any vegetables to go with it, but in this recipe *tare* (teriyaki sauce) flavoured crispy salmon skin is rolled with similarly crunchy cucumber and decorated by smoked salmon outside for a meaty texture.

Makes 4 rolls (32 pieces)

1 quantity sushi rice (see page 10)
100g salmon skin (skins from 4 fillets)

FOR *TARE* SAUCE:
4 tablespoons *shoyu* (soy sauce)
3 tablespoon *sake* or white wine
1 tablespoon *mirin*
1 tablespoon sugar

4 tablespoons white sesame seeds,
   lightly toasted
2 sheets *nori*, halved
5–6cm cucumber, deseeded
   and shredded
4 thin slices smoked salmon
   (about 150g)

TO GARNISH:
renkon (lotus root) slices or
   Onuga (reformed herring roe) or
   capers, crushed
lemon wedges
vinegared ginger (see page 8)
shoyu (soy sauce)

1 Make the sushi rice. Meanwhile, prepare the filling ingredients. You can use leftover grilled salmon skin, but if you are taking skins from fresh salmon fillets, keep a little meat on the skin. Grill the skin under a moderate heat for 3–4 minutes on each side until crisp. Remove and chop into small pieces.

2 Mix the *tare* ingredients in a small saucepan and bring to a boil over a moderate heat stirring all the time. Lower the heat and simmer for about 10 minutes until reduced to half. Remove from the heat and marinate the salmon skin pieces in it for 10–15 minutes. Drain and leave to cool. (The juice can be used as teriyaki sauce.)

3 Prepare a *uramaki* rice bed following the recipe on page 18, and sprinkle 1 tablespoonful toasted sesame seeds over. Turn over onto a cling film wrapped *makisu* crossways in parallel with you. Put a quarter of the salmon skin in a row on the *nori*, 2–3cm inside the edge nearest you. Add a quarter of the shredded cucumber.

4 Roll the *makisu* according to the method shown on page 18. Unroll the *makisu*.

5 Make up a rectangular piece (about 18 x 5cm) of smoked salmon from a slice, and cover the salmon skin roll. Place the cling film-covered *makisu* over the roll, and gently press into a round shape. Remove the roll from the *makisu*.

6 Make 3 more rolls using the remaining ingredients. Cut each roll into 8 pieces, and arrange on a serving plate with the smoked salmon side up, garnished with half a *renkon* slice, or a dot of Onuga or crushed capers on top, and with lemon wedges and vinegared ginger. Serve with *shoyu* in a small dish, or individual dishes.

futomaki (large rolls)

A speciality of the Osaka area, *futomaki* usually uses five ingredients
with contrasting colours wrapped up by a whole sheet of *nori*, as opposed
to a half sheet for *hosomaki* (thin rolls). It makes a beautiful party dish.

Makes 3 rolls (24 pieces) to serve 4
as part of a main course

1 quantity sushi rice (see page 10)
1 *tamago-yaki* (thick omelette,
   see page 11)
6 stalks asparagus or long stem
   broccoli, trimmed
1 carrot, peeled

FOR THE MUSHROOMS:
5–6 dried shiitake mushrooms,
   soaked in water for at least 1 hour

FOR THE HAND VINEGAR:
1 cup (250ml) water
2 tablespoons rice vinegar

3 sheets *nori* (20 x 18cm)
8 seafood sticks
vinegared ginger (see page 8)
shoyu (soy sauce)

1 Make the sushi rice. Meanwhile, prepare the filling ingredients.
Make the *tamago-yaki* (thick omelette), and when cool cut into about
1cm square sticks. You need a total length of 60cm.

2 Cook the asparagus in lightly salted boiling water for 7–8 minutes
until tender. If using long stem broccoli cook for 2–4 minutes. Drain
and cool under running water. Leave to drain.

3 Cook the carrot and the shiitake following the instructions on
page 8.

4 Place a *nori* on a *makisu* (rolling mat), wet your hands in the hand
vinegar, and then follow the instructions on page 17, but use two
amounts of sushi rice to cover the *nori* sheet, and leave about 3cm
margin on the furthest side. Make the rice bed fairly thick.

5 Put 2½ seafood sticks in a row across on the centre of the rice.
Put the *tamago-yaki* beside it, and then 2 asparagus stalks or broccoli
florets, some carrot and shiitake across on top of the seafood sticks
and *tamago-yaki*.

6 Roll the sushi according to the instructions on page 17. Repeat to
make two more rolls with the remaining ingredients. Cut each roll into
8 pieces and arrange on a serving plate, garnished with vinegared
ginger. Serve with a little *shoyu* in individual plates.

temaki (hand roll)

This is a DIY sushi, a perfect dinner party dish! Serve the prepared ingredients on a plate together with the vinegared rice and *nori* sheets on the table and let the guests hand-roll their own. The following are the most commonly used ingredients, but choose your own with varied tastes, textures and colours.

Makes approximately 12 rolls

1 quantity sushi rice (see page 10)
2 large king crab leg meat pieces or
    3 seafood sticks, cut lengthways
    into thin strips
70g smoked salmon, sliced into
    thin strips
1 thin egg sheet (page 11), cut into
    5–6cm long strips
6cm piece cucumber, deseeded and
    cut into 3–5mm thick sticks
6cm piece *takuan* (pickled daikon),
    cut into 3–5mm thick sticks
handful *enoki* mushroom, trimmed,
    optional
4 sheets *nori*, each cut into half or 4,
    and/or some iceberg lettuce cups

TO GARNISH:
vinegared ginger (see page 8)
wasabi
shoyu (soy sauce)

1 Make the sushi rice. Transfer the sushi rice to a serving bowl.

2 Arrange the crab leg meat, smoked salmon, egg sheet strips, cucumber, *takuan* and *enoki*, if using, on a separate serving platter. Serve them with the *nori* and the lettuce cups, if using, with the vinegared ginger in a separate dish.

3 Diners take a sheet of *nori*, or a lettuce cup, onto their individual plates and roll their own *temaki* using the sushi rice and choosing any filling ingredients they like. Serve with the vinegared ginger, *wasabi* and *shoyu*.

tamago-maki (egg sheet roll)

Using a thin egg sheet instead of *nori* for rolling makes this a very
attractive sushi. You can use any filling you like, even sausages or cheese.
Here I have tried a vegetarian one – long stem broccoli combined by
the distinct flavour of *hijiki* (black sprig seaweed).

Makes 4 rolls (24 pieces)

1 quantity sushi rice (see page 10)
2 tablespoons white sesame seeds,
   lightly toasted
4 thin egg sheets (see page 11)
2–3 tablespoons dried *hijiki*,
   soaked in water for 20 minutes
100ml soup stock (fish, chicken
   or vegetable)
8 spears long stem broccoli

TO GARNISH:
vinegared ginger (see page 8)
shoyu (soy sauce)

1   Make the sushi rice, and fold in the sesame seeds. Make the 4 thin
egg sheets.

2   Cook the *hijiki* following the recipe (how to cook vegetables)
on page 8 but substitute the stock for the shiitake soaking liquid, and
omit the *sake*.

3   Cook the broccoli spears in lightly salted boiling water
for 2 minutes until soft but still crunchy; drain and pat dry with
kitchen paper.

4   Trim 2cm from the right and left edge of each egg sheet and place
on a cutting board. Spread a quarter of the sushi rice evenly over
the egg sheet, leaving a 2cm margin at the far end. Put a broccoli spear
crossways in the centre of the rice and a quarter of the *hijiki* next to
it. Roll in the same way as other *maki-zushi* (see page 17). Paste some
crushed rice on the edge to make it stick.

5   Repeat this process to make 3 more rolls using the remaining
ingredients. Cut each roll into 6–8 pieces, and arrange on a serving
platter, garnished with vinegared ginger. Serve with the *shoyu* in
small individual dishes.

nigiri-zushi (hand-moulded sushi with ingredients on top)

The key to success in making *nigiri*, otherwise a chef's job, is to make all the finger rice moulded to an equal size and shape. I suggest you measure the rice using a tablespoon as precisely as possible.

assorted traditional *nigiri*

This assortment of toppings is only a suggestion based on the traditional ingredients – use your imagaination and make your own. (*Kabayaki*, grilled and flavoured eel, is available frozen at Japanese shops.)

Makes 24–28 pieces

½ quantity sushi rice (see page 10)
4 fresh king prawns
150g fresh tuna fillet, skinned
150g fresh salmon fillet, skinned

FOR THE MARINADE:
4 tablespoons *shoyu* (soy sauce)
2 tablespoons red wine
2 teaspoons *mirin*

1 small (approx 75g) fresh turbot
    or lemon sole fillet, skinned, and
    cut in half lengthways
lime juice
1 small fillet cured mackerel (see
    page 46) or 2 pickled herring fillets
1 *unagi kabayaki* (grilled eel), thawed
1 *tamago-yaki* (thick omelette, see
    page 11), cut into 4

TO GARNISH:
wasabi paste
small piece of *nori*
strips of *shiso* leaf
Onuga (reformed herring egg roe) or
    lumpfish caviar
kinome or lemon thyme
1 thin slice lime, cut into 4
1 small piece ginger, finely shredded
1 spring onion, finely shredded
vinegared ginger (see page 8)
shoyu (soy sauce)

1 Make the sushi rice. Meanwhile prepare the topping ingredients.

2 Remove the head of the prawns, devein and skewer following the method on page 8. Blanch the prawns in boiling water for about 2 minutes until the shell is bright red. Drain and place under running water. Remove the skewers, shell the prawns, then make a slit on the belly lengthways and open up.

3 Slice the tuna and salmon into neat sashimi pieces, measuring 1 x 4 x 7cm, making 4 pieces of each. Marinate in a mixture of the marinade ingredients for 3–4 minutes, remove onto kitchen paper and pat dry.

4 Slice the turbot or lemon sole from the thick end in 4 *sashimi* pieces about 7cm long. Make a cross slit in the centre of each, and sprinkle with lime juice.

5 Slice the cured mackerel fillets slightly diagonally into 4cm wide pieces to make 4 pieces. Cut the *kabayaki* in half lengthways, then again crossways to make 2 pieces about 7cm long. Make a slit lengthways in the centre to make it flexible.

6 Make 4 prawn *nigiri* following the steps opposite. Then make 4 each of tuna, salmon, turbot, mackerel and *kabayaki* (without *wasabi*). When making the omelette-topped *nigiri*, do not use *wasabi* but tie the whole with a thin *nori* ribbon. Tie the turbot with a similarly thin ribbon made from a *shiso* leaf.

7 Garnish with a tiny amount of Onuga on top of the prawn *nigiri*, *kinome* (or lemon thyme) on the tuna, a tiny slice of lime on the turbot, and shredded ginger on the mackerel. On the *kabayaki* brush with the *kabayaki* sauce which comes in the packet. Arrange on a serving plate, or 7 pieces each on 4 individual plates, garnished with vinegared ginger and serve with a little *shoyu* and some additional *wasabi*.

how make *nigiri*

1 Take a tablespoonful of the sushi rice in one hand, and mould into a 1.5 x 1.5 x 3cm rectangular finger sushi. Holding the topping in your other hand, paste a tiny amount of *wasabi* on top.

2 Place the rice carefully onto the topping and press gently together.

3 Turn it over and finally shape into a neat *nigiri* with the topping uppermost.

modern tuna *nigiri*

Sushi chefs never stop inventing new sushi using new, modern ingredients, but *nigiri* is probably the least explored because of its simplicity. Traditional ingredients such as raw fish and shellfish still dominate, but now grilled or part grilled fish are very popular in Japan as well as abroad.

Makes 12 pieces

¼ quantity sushi rice (see page 10)
450g fresh tuna or salmon fillet, skinned
balsamic vinegar
salt and freshly ground black pepper
1 spring onion, finely shredded
2 teaspoons mayonnaise
½ clove garlic, grated
shoyu (soy sauce)
½ red onion, finely shredded
2 lemon slices, cut into pieces

FOR THE SAUCE:
1 tablespoon lemon juice
1 tablespoon extra virgin olive oil
1 teaspoon *shoyu* (soy sauce)

TO GARNISH:
parsley
vinegared ginger (see page 8)

1 Make the sushi rice. Meanwhile prepare the topping ingredients.

2 Slice the tuna neatly into 12 *sashimi* pieces, measuring 7 x 3 x 5cm. Make crisscross slits on one side of 4 pieces, and very lightly grill on the side with the slits under a high heat for a few seconds. Remove from the heat, and brush with some balsamic vinegar.

3 Grill another 4 pieces on one side only, and using a hot metal skewer make a crisscross burned pattern on the grilled side.

4 Following the method on page 35, make 4 *nigiri* each with the balsamic flavoured tuna, the patterned tuna and the raw tuna. Brush some more balsamic vinegar on the vinegar flavoured tuna, sprinkle with salt and pepper and garnish with finely shredded spring onion on top. Make 3 more in the same way.

5 For the grilled tuna with the burnt pattern, mix the mayonnaise, grated garlic and a few drops of *shoyu*, and put a dot of the mixture on top.

6 For the raw tuna, mix the red onion shreds and the lemon pieces, and put a quarter of the mixture on top of each. Mix the sauce ingredients, season with salt and pepper, and sprinkle over the onion mixture. Garnish with a sprig of parsley on top.

7 Arrange all the *nigiri* on a serving plate, garnish with the vinegared ginger and serve.

gunkan-maki (battleship roll)

This battleship shaped *nigiri-zushi* is the easiest to make. Simply wrap a *nori* ribbon round a finger of rice, and put fillings on top. The two most commonly used fillings are *ikura* (salmon caviar) and sea urchin. Use readily available fillings such as Onuga (reformed herring egg roe) or lumpfish caviar, dressed crab as well as salmon caviar as in this recipe. Instead of the traditional *nori*, strips of daikon (mooli, long white radish) can be used for wrapping.

Makes 12 pieces

½ quantity sushi rice (see page 10)
1 large daikon (mooli, white radish), peeled and cut in 3cm slices
1 cup (250ml) water plus 2 tablespoons salt
4 okra, trimmed and cooked
2 tablespoons Onuga (reformed herring roe) or lumpfish caviar
1 sheet *nori*
40g dressed crab
1–2 spring onions, finely chopped
pinch hot chilli powder, optional
a few drops *shoyu* (soy sauce) plus extra for serving
kinome or lemon thyme
40g *ikura* (salmon caviar)
chopped chives
wasabi
vinegared ginger (see page 8) to garnish
lime juice

1 Make the sushi rice. Meanwhile prepare the remaining ingredients.

2 Using a wide peeler, make 4 thin daikon strips about 15cm long. Soak the daikon strips in the mixture of the water and salt for 10 minutes until soft. Drain and pat dry with kitchen paper.

3 Finely chop the cooked okra and mix with the Onuga or lumpfish caviar. Take a tablespoonful of the sushi rice in hand, and mould into a 5 x 2 x 2cm rectangular finger of rice. Wrap a daikon strip around the rice, and fill with a quarter of the okra and caviar mixture. Make 3 more daikon *gunkan-maki*.

4 Cut the *nori* sheet into 8 ribbons about 15 x 3cm. Mix the dressed crab and the spring onion and season with hot chilli, if using, and *shoyu* to taste. Make 4 more finger rice and wrap a *nori* ribbon around. Fill with the dressed crab mixture, and garnish with a sprig of *kinome* or lemon thyme.

5 Make another 4 finger rice and wrap a *nori* sheet around the rice. Fill with salmon caviar and garnish with the mixture of chopped chives and *wasabi* on top.

6 Arrange on a serving plate garnished with vinegared ginger, and serve with the lime juice and a little *shoyu* in small dishes.

kikka-zushi (chrysanthemum flower sushi)

In Japanese cuisine dishes are meant to please the eyes as well as the palate, and this applies not only to the *haute cuisine* but also to everyday home cooking including sushi. Cooks therefore try to recreate the most beautiful aspects of nature. This stunningly beautiful sushi is created in the image of a chrysanthemum flower, Japan's national flower, and is ideal for an autumn party.

Makes 12 pieces

½ quantity sushi rice (see page 10)
6 giant prawns in shells

FOR THE MARINADE:
3 tablespoons *sake*
3 tablespoons rice vinegar
1 teaspoon *shoyu* (soy sauce)
1 teaspoon *mirin* or sugar

1 hardboiled egg yolk

TO GARNISH:
chrysanthemum leaves or watercress
vinegared ginger (see page 8)
shoyu (soy sauce)

1 Make the sushi rice. Meanwhile, prepare the ingredients.

2 Remove the heads and devein the prawns following the method on page 8. Tightly curl the prawns and fix each with a cocktail stick. Cook in lightly salted boiling water for 2 minutes until the shells are bright red, and drain. Remove the coctail sticks, peel, and slice each prawn into two rings. Mix all the marinade ingredients in a shallow dish and marinate the prawns for 10 minutes. Drain.

3 Place a prawn, shell-side down, on a sheet of cling film, about 20 x 20cm. Spoon a heaped tablespoonful of rice onto your hand and shape to a small ball. Put it on top of the prawn, and wrap the cling film around the rice to make a slightly flat ball. Carefully shape into a chrysanthemum flower. Repeat to make 5 more chrysanthemum sushi.

4 Sieve the boiled egg yolk through a fine mesh. Put a small amount of egg yolk crumbled on the centre of the prawns. Arrange on a serving plate, garnished with some chrysanthemum leaves or watercress around the sushi. Serve with vinegared ginger and *shoyu* in a small dish.

oshi-zushi (pressed sushi)

Sushi rice with toppings are pressed in a container, and cut into pieces: pressed sushi is a very convenient way to make multiple sushi at one go, hence ideal for a party. Moreover, it keeps up to 36 hours, so you can make it a day in advance.

masu-zushi (smoked trout pressed sushi)

Normally, cooked or cured seafood or pickled vegetables are used for pressed sushi, and cured trout is one of the traditional toppings. Here more readily available smoked trout is used. You can also use smoked salmon. (SEE PAGE 42.)

Makes 1 box of 15 x 15cm (16 pieces)

1 quantity sushi rice (see page 10)
170g smoked trout, or smoked salmon, thickly sliced
2 tablespoons *shoyu* (soy sauce) plus extra to serve
2 tablespoons *sake*
2 tablespoons black or white sesame seeds, lightly toasted
finely grated zest of 1 lemon

FOR THE HAND VINEGAR:
1 cup (250ml) water
2 tablespoons rice vinegar

TO GARNISH:
2 slices lime
Onuga (reformed herring roe) or lumpfish caviar
vinegared ginger (see page 8)

1 Make the sushi rice. Meanwhile prepare the other ingredients. Marinate the smoked fish slices in the mixture of the *shoyu* and *sake* for 10 minutes, then drain and pat dry with a kitchen paper. Sprinkle the sesame seeds over the sushi rice, and lightly fold in – do not mash.

2 Prepare the mould or box as in Step 3 opposite. Lay the smoked fish slices evenly in the bottom and sprinkle the lemon zest on top.

3 Wet your hands in the hand-vinegar, take a handful of rice and press into a ball, then press it down on the fish. Repeat to cover all the fish evenly. Cover the mould or box as in Step 4 opposite. Leave in a cool place (but never in the refrigerator) for a few hours or overnight.

4 Remove from the container, unwrap, and cut into bite-size pieces using a sharp knife and wiping the knife with vinegar-soaked kitchen paper after each cut. Arrange on a large serving plate, and garnish with a small fan-shaped lime slice and Onuga or lumpfish caviar on top of each piece. Serve with vinegared ginger and a little *shoyu* in individual dishes.

kani-zushi (crabmeat pressed sushi)

Ekiben (station bento) is a must to taste on your railway journey in Japan, and each station has their own speciality using their local produce. Crab is the speciality of the north, but *kani-zushi* or *kani-bento* is one of the most commonly available lunch boxes throughout Japan. It's very easy to make and delicious to eat. (SEE PAGE 43.)

Makes 1 box (15 x 15cm), 16 pieces

½ quantity sushi rice (see page 10)
200g crabmeat from 2 cooked fresh
 crabs, or tinned, flaked
1 tablespoon lemon juice
salt and freshly ground black pepper
100g jarred cooked langoustine meat
 or 70g smoked salmon
2 thin egg sheets (see page 11),
 finely shredded
kinome or lemon thyme
vinegared ginger (see page 8)
shoyu (soy sauce)

1   Make the sushi rice.

2   If using tinned crabmeat, heat a small saucepan over moderate heat, add the crabmeat and vigorously stir until it becomes flaky. Add the lemon juice and season with salt and pepper. Cut each langoustine body in half lengthways.

3   Line a wooden sushi mould, or a square shallow container (approximately 15 x 15cm) with cling film, and spread the sushi rice evenly over the base, pressing firmly, and add a layer of langoustine pieces or smoked salmon to cover the rice. Layer the crabmeat evenly on top and press firmly.

4   Sprinkle the shreds of thin egg sheet over, and cover with a wooden lid. If using a plastic box, cut cardboard into a square to fit inside the box, and place on the cling film on top of the sushi. Place a weight on top and leave pressed until ready to serve. (This can be made up to 36 hours in advance but sushi should never be kept in the refrigerator.)

5   Remove from the container, and cut into bite-size pieces wiping the blade with vinegar-soaked kitchen paper after each cut. Garnish with *kinome* or lemon thyme, and serve with vinegared ginger and *shoyu*.

battera (mackerel log-shaped sushi)

Battera, now a fixture at any sushi restaurant around the world, is originally from Osaka. You can make it in a container in the same way as the smoked trout sushi on the previous page, but making it in a log-shape using a piece of fillet for each is a more authentic *battera*. Traditionally this would have been wrapped in dried bamboo bark as pictured below but clingfilm works well to keep it moist.

Makes 2 *battera* (16–18 pieces)

1 large fresh mackerel (about 450g), filleted
salt
1 piece *konbu* (dried kelp), about 10 x 5cm, optional
1 quantity sushi rice (see page 10)
3–4 tablespoons rice vinegar
clingfilm or sheets of bamboo bark

TO GARNISH:
lemon wedges
vinegared ginger (see page 8)
wasabi paste
shoyu (soy sauce)

1 Start the preparation the night before. Place the mackerel fillets, skin side down, on a thick bed of salt in a shallow flat dish, cover completely with more salt and leave refrigerated overnight.

2 Before cooking rice, soak the *konbu* in the water in which the rice will be cooked, for 3–4 hours to flavour it, if you like. Discard the *konbu* and make the sushi rice using the flavoured water.

3 Wash the salt off the mackerel fillets under running water and pat dry with kitchen paper. Carefully remove all the bones with tweezers, and the blood clots from the central vein. Place the fillets in a clean, flat dish and pour the rice vinegar over. Leave for 20 minutes.

4 Using your fingers, remove the outer transparent skin from each fillet. Place the fillets, skin side down, on a cutting board and slice off the highest part to make the fillets flat. Keep the trimmings.

5 Using wet hands, and half the rice, make a firm log shape about the length of the mackerel fillets. Place the rice on a clingfilm-covered *makisu* (or place the rice on a sheet of dried bamboo bark) and put a fillet on top with the skin side up. Use the trimmings to cover the rice completely, and also under the cavity. Wrap the whole sushi with the *makisu* pressing firmly into a neat log shape. Leave wrapped in a cool place (not in the refrigerator) for a few hours, or overnight.

6 Unwrap the *battera*, and slice crossways into 2–3cm thick pieces. Divide the sushi between 4 individual plates, and serve garnished with lemon wedges, vinegared ginger and *wasabi*, with a little *shoyu* in individual dishes.

rainbow roll (*tazuna-zushi*)

Tazuna, meaning 'rein' in Japanese, is a twisted rope, and this roll has a pattern on top resembling a thick rope, and uses ingredients with various colours and tastes. It is quite a complicated sushi to make, but it will make a stunningly beautiful party dish.

Makes 3 rolls (18 pieces)

1/2 quantity sushi rice (see page 10)
2 pickled herring fillets, or rollmops
10cm cucumber
2 tablespoons salt
1 cup (250ml) water
120g smoked trout or smoked salmon

FOR THE HAND VINEGAR:
1 cup (250ml) water
2 tablespoons rice vinegar

TO GARNISH:
shiso leaves
lemon wedges
vinegared ginger (see page 8)
wasabi paste
shoyu (soy sauce)

1 Make the sushi rice. Meanwhile prepare the ingredients. Pat dry the pickled herring fillets with kitchen paper, and cut each lengthways into 2 fillets.

2 Using a wide peeler, cut about 4 very thin strips from the cucumber lengthways from one side, and repeat on a further 3 sides; discard the outer strip of peel. Add the salt to the measured water in a shallow bowl and soak the cucumber strips for 10 minutes; drain and pat dry with kitchen paper.

3 Cut the smoked trout or smoked salmon into strips about 10cm long, 3 cm wide.

4 Wet your hands in the hand vinegar, then take a third of the sushi rice (approximately 70g) and shape into a firm cylinder about 20cm long. Place on a cling film-covered *makisu*. Lay a strip of cucumber, smoked trout and pickled herring (with the silver pattern up) slightly diagonally, like a forward slash, on the rice, all slightly overlapping. Repeat this until the rice is completely covered. Cover with a cling film-covered *makisu* and press to shape. Remove from the *makisu*, and keep it wrapped in the cling film until ready to serve.

5 Repeat this process to make 2 more rolls using the remaining ingredients. Cut each roll into 6, and arrange on *shiso* leaves on a serving plate. Serve garnished with lemon wedges, vinegared ginger, and *wasabi* and with *shoyu* in individual dishes.

inari-zushi
(mixed sushi in a fried tofu parcel) - vegetarian

Abura-age (fried thin tofu), a great source of protein in old vegetarian Japan, is still a very popular item for daily cooking. Cut in half it opens up and becomes an interesting parcel for mixed sushi as shown here. *Abura-age* is available frozen at Japanese supermarkets.

Makes 6 parcels

½ quantity sushi rice (see page 10)
3 *abura-age* (pouches made
   from tofu)

FOR THE COOKING SAUCE:
100ml water
5 tablespoons *sake*
5 tablespoons sugar
2 tablespoon *shoyu* (soy sauce)
salt

2 tablespoons dried *hijiki*, soaked in
   water for 20 minutes and/or 2–3
   dried shiitake, soaked in water for
   at least 1 hour, drained
1 tablespoon sesame seeds,
   lightly toasted

TO GARNISH:
vinegared ginger (see page 8)
shoyu (soy sauce)

1 Make the sushi rice. Meanwhile prepare the other ingredients.

2 Pour plenty of boiling water over the *abura-age* to draw out the oil and then squeeze out the excess water. Cut each piece in half and carefully open up to make 6 parcels.

3 Mix all the ingredients for the cooking sauce and bring to a boil stirring to dissolve the sugar. Add the *abura-age* halves and simmer over low heat for about 10 minutes until evenly coloured amber. Remove from the heat and leave to cool in the liquid.

4 Squeeze excess water from the *hijiki* and roughly chop. If using shiitake cut off the stems and finely chop. Cook shiitake, if using, and *hijiki* following the method on page 8.

5 Roughly crush the sesame seeds using a pestle and mortar.

6 While the sushi rice is still warm, sprinkle over the sesame seeds and fold in the cooked *hijiki* and/or shiitake. Divide the mixed rice into 6 balls, stuff a ball of rice into each parcel, and then fold in the edge. You may reverse some of the tofu parcels and make inside-out *inari*. You may also cut some in half diagonally and stuff rice in the corner to make 12 half-size triangle *inari*.

7 Arrange on a serving plate garnished with vinegared ginger and serve garnished with *shoyu* in individual dishes.

inro-zushi (cucumber log sushi)

Inro, an old word for a pillbox, is one of the most sought-after items for collectors of Japanese antiques. This *inro*-shaped sushi is made with white gourd in Japan, but here I tried with English cucumber and it works beautifully.

Makes 4 half cucumber logs
   (approximately 26 pieces)

½ quantity sushi rice (see page 10)
2 English cucumbers, halved
2 tablespoons salt
1 litre water
1 piece (approx 10 x 5cm) *konbu*
   (dried kelp), optional
6 fresh tiger prawns, or
   100g cooked prawns
2 tablespoons *sake*
1 tablespoon sugar
2 teaspoons *mirin*
pinch of salt

TO GARNISH:
shoyu (soy sauce)
wasabi paste

1   Make the sushi rice. Meanwhile prepare the other ingredients.

2   Trim the cucumber halves and, using a citrus zester, cut fine peel strips on the cucumber skin lengthways, retaining the peeled skin. Chop the strips very finely.

3   Using a corer cut a neat round hole down the centre of each cucumber half. Soak the hollow cucumber halves in the mixture of the salt, water and the *konbu*, if using, for 30 minutes, drain and leave to dry. Discard the *konbu*, or use for other recipes.

4   Devein the tiger prawns following the method on page 8. Mix the *sake*, sugar, *mirin* and salt in a small saucepan and bring to the boil. Add the prawns and cook on a moderate heat for 5–6 minutes until almost all the cooking juice has been absorbed. When cool, shell and finely dice the flesh. If using cooked prawns, heat the mixture of the seasonings and marinate for 10 minutes. Drain and finely dice.

5   Fold the chopped cucumber peel and prawns in the sushi rice, and use it to firmly stuff the central hole of each cucumber half. Cut crossways into 1–2cm wide rounds. Arrange on a serving platter and serve with *shoyu* with a little *wasabi* in individual dishes.

gomoku-zushi bento (vegetarian sushi lunch box)

Gomoku-zushi, sushi rice mixed with five or more kinds of ingredients, is a very popular luncheon dish: you can feed a large number of people with just one gorgeous looking dish. It's also ideal as a bento box for you to take to work as it doesn't normally contain raw fish. For non-vegetarians add chopped smoked salmon, cooked prawns or even sausages.

Makes 2 bento boxes

1 quantity sushi rice (see page 10)
5–6cm carrot, peeled
2 dried shiitake, soaked in water
   for minimum 1 hour, soaking
   water retained
1 heaped tablespoon dried *hijiki*
   (black sprig seaweed), washed and
   soaked in water for 30 minutes,
   optional
10 mangetout, trimmed
3–4 thin slices cooked and marinated
   renkon (lotus root), optional
   (see below)
1 thin egg sheet (see page 11)
2 tablespoons white sesame seeds,
   lightly toasted

1 Make the sushi rice. Meanwhile prepare the other ingredients.

2 Cook the carrot, shiitake and *hijiki*, if using, following the recipe on page 8.

3 Cut the mangetout in half diagonally, and cook in a plenty of lightly salted boiling water for 1 minute until just soft but still crunchy, drain and refresh under running water. Pat dry with kitchen paper.

4 Cut the *renkon*, if using, in half, or quarters if large.

5 Make the thin egg sheet, and chop into fine shreds of 4–5cm long.

6 Sprinkle the sesame seeds on the sushi rice and fold in together with all the other ingredients except the egg shreds and divide between 2 lunch boxes. Garnish with the egg shreds on top. If serving as a party dish, arrange the *gomoku-zushi* in a large pasta bowl and decorate with egg shreds and some finely shredded *nori* on top if preferred. Serve warm.

Renkon (lotus root)

FOR THE MARINADE FOR
   1 SECTION RENKON:
200ml rice vinegar or white
   wine vinegar
4 tablespoons sugar or 5 tablespoons
   if using white wine vinegar
2 teaspoons salt

If using fresh *renkon*, peel, slice into thin rings, then cook in boiling water with about 1 tablespoon rice vinegar for about 5 minutes until just soft, and drain. Mix the rice vinegar, sugar and salt in a saucepan and heat over a low heat, stirring until the sugar has dissolved. Remove from the heat and leave to cool. Marinate the *renkon* for 15–20 minutes or until ready to use. The *renkon* in the marinade will keep for weeks in the refrigerator.

chirashi donburi (sushi rice bowl with tuna, salmon, prawn and vegetables)

Otherwise known as *Edo-mae* (Tokyo style) *chirashi*, this is a sushi rice bowl with ingredients on top. Traditionally just tuna is used together with cooked vegetables, but here I suggest marinated tuna, salmon and cooked prawn, mushrooms, spinach and *renkon* (lotus root). The *sashimi* are usually eaten dipped in *shoyu* and *wasabi*.

Serves 4

1½ quantities sushi rice (see page 10)
4 slices cooked *renkon*, optional
3 tablespoons rice vinegar or
    white wine vinegar
1 tablespoon sugar or 1½ if using
    white wine vinegar
250g fresh tuna fillet, skinned
250g fresh salmon fillet, skinned

FOR THE TUNA MARINADE:
4 tablespoons *shoyu* (soy sauce)
2 tablespoons red wine
2 teaspoons *mirin*

FOR THE SALMON:
2 tablespoons *shoyu* (soy sauce)
wasabi paste to taste

4 fresh tiger prawns
2 tablespoons *sake*
1 tablespoon water
1 tablespoon *mirin*
1 teaspoon *shoyu* (soy sauce)
½ quantity *tamago-yaki* omelette
    (see page 11), cut into 8 thin strips
70g *shimeji* mushrooms, trimmed
4 large dried shiitake, soaked in
    water for at least 1 hour
60g spinach, trimmed
vinegared ginger (see page 8)

1   Make the sushi rice. Meanwhile prepare the other ingredients. Slice the *renkon* into 5mm thick rounds and marinate in the mixture of the rice vinegar and sugar, if using. Set aside.

2   Slice the tuna and salmon into 8 neat *sashimi* pieces (see page 8), about 5 x 3–4 x 3cm. Marinate the tuna and salmon in their marinades for 5–10 minutes and drain.

3   Pull the heads off the prawns and devein following the method on page 8. Tightly curl the prawns and fix with a bamboo skewer or cocktail stick. Mix the *sake*, water, *mirin* and *shoyu* in a small saucepan and bring to the boil. Add the prawns and cook over a moderate heat for 3–4 minutes. Remove from the heat and leave to cool in the cooking juice. When cool, carefully remove the skewers and peel the prawns.

4   Cook the *shimeji* in lightly salted boiling water for 1 minute and drain. Drain the shiitake, retaining the soaking water, and trim off the stems. Cook following the recipe on page 8. Remove from the heat, drain and leave to cool, retaining the liquid. Marinate the cooked *shimeji* in the remaining shiitake liquid for a moment just to flavour.

5   Boil the spinach in lightly salted boiling water for 30 seconds, drain and immediately refresh under running water. Squeeze out excess water and sprinkle with a little *shoyu*. Shape into a 7–8cm long log and cut into 4 crossways.

6   Divide the sushi rice between 4 individual bowls and arrange equal amounts of tuna, salmon, prawns, *tamago-yaki* strips, *shimeji* and shiitake mushrooms, spinach rounds, and *renkon*, if using, prettily to cover the rice. Serve garnished with some vinagared ginger.

seared swordfish *sashimi* salad with *miso* vinegar dressing

Sashimi salad is one of the most popular fusion dishes at Japanese restaurants outside Japan as it makes an easy starting point for newcomers to the art of eating fish raw. At home, if you can't get *sashimi* quality fresh fish to eat completely raw, I suggest you either sear or blanch raw fish as in this recipe.

Serves 4

500g fresh swordfish fillet, skinned
½ onion
120g mixed salad leaves

FOR THE DRESSING:
2½ tablespoons white *miso*
  (soya paste)
1½ tablespoons rice vinegar or
   white wine vinegar
2 tablespoons *sake* or white wine
1–2 teaspoons mustard

TO GARNISH:
sesame seeds, lightly toasted

1 Quickly sear the swordfish on both sides until only the surface is cooked and the centre is still pink. Slice thinly crossways, inserting the blade slightly diagonally.

2 Slice the onion into very thin half-moons and put in ice water to freshen and to reduce some sharpness. Drain and pat dry with a kitchen paper. Mix with the salad leaves.

3 Mix the dressing and put some in the centre of each of 4 individual plates. Arrange a quarter of the salad on top, and a quarter of the swordfish slices around the salad. Drizzle the remaining dressing over the fish, sprinkle with sesame seeds and serve.

sunomono (vinegared salad) **with cucumber, *wakame* (young sea leaves), and octopus**

In place of, or together with, vinegared ginger, why not try a *sunomono* to accompany sushi? It refreshes the palate just as the vinegared ginger does, and is absolutely delicious. Cucumber and *wakame* are the two regular ingredients for *sunomono* and octopus gives it an added texture as well as a rich taste.

Serves 4–6

½ cucumber
salt
10g dried *wakame*, soaked in water
　　for 20 minutes
1 tentacle octopus
1 piece (about 3cm square) fresh
　　ginger, peeled and finely shredded

FOR THE DRESSING:
1 tablespoon rice vinegar or
　　white wine vinegar
1 teaspoon sugar
1 teaspoon *mirin*
1 teaspoon *shoyu* (soy sauce)

1　Using a citrus zester, make fine stripes lengthways on the cucumber skin and discard the skin strips. Cut the cucumber in half lengthways and slice very thinly. Spread the slices on large flat plate and sprinkle with salt. Leave for 5 minutes until they wilt, and then using your hands squeeze out the excess water.

2　Drain the *wakame* and, using your hands, squeeze out the excess water. Pour boiling water over to freshen and make the green vivid. Squeeze out the excess water again and chop into bite-size pieces.

3　Cook the octopus tentacle in boiling water over a moderate heat for 15 minutes until tender, remove from the heat and refresh under running water. Slice into very thin discs.

4　Put the ginger shreds in iced water to freshen and to reduce the sharpness. Drain.

5　Mix all the dressing ingredients in a small cup and stir well until the sugar has dissolved.

6　Mix the cucumber, *wakame* and octopus in a mixing bowl and, just before serving, pour the vinegar dressing over. Divide between individual plates and serve garnished with a few ginger shreds on top.

sushi salad

Sushi is a food for all seasons, but in hot and humid summer when you don't have much appetite sushi is particularly appealing due to the refreshing vinegary taste. This recipe combines a summer salad with sushi, accentuating the vinegar content very nicely.

Serves 4–6

1 quantity sushi rice (see page 10)
8–12 tiger prawns
1 medium fresh squid, cleaned
 and skinned

FOR THE SALAD DRESSING:
1 tablespoon white wine vinegar
3 tablespoons extra virgin olive oil
1–2 teaspoons mustard

½ cucumber
12 baby plum tomatoes, halved
3 iceberg lettuce leaves, torn into
 small pieces
handful chard or opal (red) basil
 leaves, optional
5 tablespoons white sesame seeds,
 lightly toasted

1 Make the sushi rice. Meanwhile prepare the other ingredients.

2 Pull off the heads and devein the prawns following the method on page 8. Cook in lightly salted boiling water over a high heat for 2–3 minutes, drain and refresh under running water. When cool enough to handle, carefully peel.

3 Cut the squid in half lengthways and make fine cross slits on the inside. Cut into pieces about 3 x 4cm and cook in lightly salted boiling water over a high heat for 1–2 minutes. Drain and refresh under running water. Pat dry with kitchen paper. Mix the salad dressing ingredients and sprinkle 1 tablespoon of dressing over.

4 Roughly peel the cucumber, keeping some green on, cut in half and de-seed. Chop into bite-size pieces. Put the cucumber, tomatoes, lettuce and chard or opal basil leaves, if using, in a bowl. Chill all the ingredients except the rice until ready to serve.

5 Sprinkle the sesame seeds on the sushi rice and lightly fold in. Divide the rice between 4 individual bowls; toss the salad in the remaining dressing and divide between the bowls, arranging it on top of the rice. Add a quarter of the prawns and squid to each bowl and serve.

glossary + index Page numbers in **BOLD** indicate recipes

a

abura-age (pouches made from fried thin tofu) 51
aji (horse mackerel)

b

battera (mackerel log-shaped sushi) **46**
bonito (dried fish, sold in blocks or very thin flakes)

c

California roll **21**
chirashi donburi (sushi rice bowl with tuna, salmon, prawn and vegetables) **56**
chirashi-zushi (scattered sushi) **43**

d

daikon (mooli, long white radish) 9
dashi (soup stock)

e

enoki (mushroom)

f

futomaki (large rolls) **26**

g

gomoku-zushi bento (vegetarian sushi lunch box) **55**
gunkan-maki (battleship roll) **39**

h

handai (wooden *sumeshi* tub) 7
hashi (Japanese chopsticks) 7
hijiki (black sprig seaweed) 7,8
hosomaki (thin rolls) with three colours **16**

i

ikura (salmon caviar)

inari-zushi (mixed sushi in a fried tofu parcel) **51**
inro-zushi (cucumber log sushi) **52**

k

kabayaki (eel)
kakiage 'spider roll' (vegetable tempura roll) **22**
kani-zushi (crabmeat pressed sushi) **45**
kanten (agar-agar, a gelling agent)
kikka-zushi (chrysanthemum flower sushi) **40**
kinome (shoots of the anise pepper tree)
konbu (dried kelp) 7

m

makisu (bamboo sushi mat) 7
maki-zushi (rolled sushi) 15, 17
masu-zushi (smoked trout pressed sushi) **44**
mirin (sweet rice wine) 7
miso (soya paste) 13
miso soup with tofu and *nameko* **12**
mitsuba (Japanese parsley)

n

nameko (mushroom) 13
nigiri, assorted traditional **35**
modern tuna **36**
nigiri-zushi (hand-moulded sushi) 33
nori (sheets made from seaweed) 7
heating over a flame 17
norimaki (*nori* rolled sushi) 15, 16

o

Onuga (reformed herring egg roe)
oshi-zushi press 7

r

rainbow roll (*tazuna-zushi*) **48**

renkon (lotus root), marinating **55**

s

sake (rice wine) 7
salmon skin roll **24**
sansho leaf (Japanese spice)
sashimi (raw seafood, sliced thinly)
seared swordfish *sashimi* salad with *miso* vinegar dressing **58**
shiso (a member of the mint family)
shoyu (soy sauce) 7
sumeshi (sushi rice) **10**
sunomono (vinegared salad) with cucumber, *wakame* (young sea leaves), and octopus **61**
sushi salad **62**

t

takuan (pickled *daikon*) 7, 9
tamago-maki (egg sheet roll) **30**
tamago-usuyaki (thin egg sheet) **11**
tamago-yaki (thick omelette) **11**
pan 7
tare (teriyaki sauce) **24**
temaki (hand roll) **29**
tobiko (fish roe)
tri-colour *maki* a l'Italia **17**

u

unagi kabayaki (grilled eel)
uramaki ebi-fry roll (reverse roll with fried prawn) **19**
uramaki-zushi, how to make 18
ushio-jiru (clear soup with clams) **12**

v, w

vinegared ginger **8**
wakame (young sea leaves)
wasabi (made from edible root, similar to horseradish) 9